D1410969

BLUE BANNER
BIOGRAPHY

David WRIGHT

Mary Boone

Mitchell Lane
PUBLISHERS

P.O. Box 196
Hockessin, Delaware 19707
Visit us on the web: www.mitchelllane.com
Comments? email us: mitchelllane@mitchelllane.com

Mitchell Lane
PUBLISHERS

Printing   1   2   3   4   5   6   7   8   9

Blue Banner Biographies

Alicia Keys	Flo Rida	Megan Fox
Allen Iverson	Gwen Stefani	Miguel Tejada
Ashanti	Ice Cube	Nancy Pelosi
Ashlee Simpson	Ja Rule	Natasha Bedingfield
Ashton Kutcher	Jamie Foxx	Orianthi
Avril Lavigne	Jay-Z	Orlando Bloom
Beyoncé	Jennifer Lopez	P. Diddy
Blake Lively	Jessica Simpson	Peyton Manning
Bow Wow	J. K. Rowling	Pink
Brett Favre	Joe Flacco	Queen Latifah
Britney Spears	John Legend	Rihanna
Carrie Underwood	Justin Berfield	Robert Pattinson
Chris Brown	Justin Timberlake	Ron Howard
Chris Daughtry	Kanye West	Sean Kingston
Christina Aguilera	Kate Hudson	Selena
Ciara	Keith Urban	Shakira
Clay Aiken	Kelly Clarkson	Shia LaBeouf
Cole Hamels	Kenny Chesney	Shontelle Layne
Condoleezza Rice	Kristen Stewart	Soulja Boy Tell 'Em
Corbin Bleu	Lady Gaga	Stephenie Meyer
Daniel Radcliffe	Lance Armstrong	Taylor Swift
David Ortiz	Leona Lewis	T.I.
David Wright	Lil Wayne	Timbaland
Derek Jeter	Lindsay Lohan	Tim McGraw
Drew Brees	Mariah Carey	Toby Keith
Eminem	Mario	Usher
Eve	Mary J. Blige	Vanessa Anne Hudgens
Fergie	Mary-Kate and Ashley Olsen	Zac Efron

Library of Congress Cataloging-in-Publication Data
Boone, Mary, 1963–
  David Wright / by Mary Boone.
    p. cm. — (Blue banner biographies)
  Includes bibliographical references and index.
  ISBN 978-1-58415-910-0 (library bound)
 1. Wright, David, 1982– —Juvenile literature. 2. Baseball players—United States—Biography—Juvenile literature. 3. Infielders (Baseball—United States—Biography—Juvenile literature. 4. New York Mets (Baseball team)—Juvenile literature. I. Title.
 GV865.W74B66 2011
 796.357092—dc22
 [B]
                                                            2010014891

ABOUT THE AUTHOR: Mary Boone is the author of more than a dozen books for young people, including Mitchell Lane biographies about Corbin Bleu, 50 Cent, and Vanessa Anne Hudgens. Mary lives in Tacoma, Washington., where she and her son, Eli, cheer on the Mariners. Her husband, Mitch, and daughter, Eve, root for the White Sox. They all agree David Wright is one of the good guys.

PUBLISHER'S NOTE: The following story has been thoroughly researched, and to the best of our knowledge represents a true story. While every possible effort has been made to ensure accuracy, the publisher will not assume liability for damages caused by inaccuracies in the data and makes no warranty on the accuracy of the information contained herein. This story has not been authorized or endorsed by David Wright.

Blue Banner Biography

David Wright's aggressive fielding earned him National League Gold Glove Awards in 2007 and 2008, but the third baseman says it's just as important to focus on the routine plays as on the spectacular ones.

Competitor from the Start

*B*rian Giles was robbed. There were 46,000 people in the stands — and most of them jumped to their feet and cheered.

It all happened during the seventh inning of a game between the New York Mets and San Diego Padres back in 2005. The Mets were trailing 6-3 with one out when Padres outfielder Brian Giles broke his bat on a 2-2 pitch, sending what looked like a base hit toward left field. Cliff Floyd raced in, while third baseman David Wright turned and sprinted straight back. At the last second, Wright jumped, grabbed the ball with his bare right hand, and held on tight as his body slammed to the ground.

The Mets didn't win the game, but Wright stole the show — and Giles' hit. The catch made its way onto sports highlights reels, and online voters named it MLB.com's Play of the Year.

That competitive, give-it-all-you've-got spirit has been the hallmark of Wright's career. It's that need to succeed that has propelled a Little Leaguer from southeast Virginia to a starring role in one of the National League's most popular franchises.

David Wright (far right) has been a fan favorite since he joined the Mets organization. In 2006, he was named to his first All-Star team and became the 13th player in history to homer in his first All-Star at-bat. Fellow Mets joining him on that team were, left to right, Carlos Beltran, Tom Glavine, Jose Reyes, and Paul Lo Duca.

Sportswriters hail Wright as a great all-around player, a solid fielder, a fast runner, and a patient batter. Countless news articles relay stories of his good looks, charm, dedication, and strong work ethic. After just five seasons in the majors, Wright set a record for the most starts by a third baseman in Mets franchise history, earned two Gold Glove Awards, two Silver Slugger trophies, and had been named to four All-Star teams.

It's clear: David Wright is the real deal.

Wright was born December 20, 1982, in Norfolk, Virginia. He grew up in Chesapeake, a suburb of the city. His father, Rhon, was a police officer; his mother, Elisa, was a teacher.

With the Mets Triple-A team, The Tides, based in Norfolk, it was natural for Wright to become a baseball fan at an early age. Rhon told *Sports Illustrated* that attending games and waiting for autographs made his son appreciate both the sport and small acts of kindness.

"David saw firsthand that it was easier to get the signature of a mascot or a batboy than a top prospect," he said. "He saw that it doesn't take much to sign a program and that a gesture of goodwill goes a long way."

Wright got his own start playing baseball with a Little League team called the Green Run Padres. With his father as the coach, David hoped for a chance to play shortstop. Instead, his dad put him in the position he hated most: right field.

"David was good at short," Rhon told *Sports Illustrated*, "but I told him he had to earn his spot in the field and prove he could make the plays. The idea of putting David in right was to instill humility."

"[David] saw that it doesn't take much to sign a program and that a gesture of goodwill goes a long way." —Rhon Wright

Rhon's plan apparently worked. David put in hours at the batting cages and played catch every chance he could. As a teenager, he joined an Amateur Athletic Union (AAU) team and then went on to become a star at Hickory High School, where he continued to be known for his dedication to the game. He even made a ritual of parking his car near the field with its headlights on so that he could take extra grounders and play pepper after dark. The extra effort paid off.

Wright makes a play in the Major League Baseball Futures Game in July 2004. His rise through the minor league system was swift. He graduated from high school in 2001 and three years later was called up to the big leagues.

Wright was selected to three All-State Baseball Teams during his high school career. As a senior, he batted .538 and was named Gatorade Virginia Player of the Year in 2001.

Later that year, the New York Mets selected him in the first round of the Major League Baseball draft. He'd already been awarded a baseball college scholarship to Georgia Tech—but he decided to pass up the free ride in favor of a rookie-level assignment in Kingsport, Tennessee. It was not exactly the big show, but it was professional baseball, and that was a step toward fulfilling a lifelong dream.

Minor League, Major Effort

*L*ife in the minor leagues is not glamorous. Young baseball players earn such small paychecks that four or more guys will often share the rent on one bare-bones apartment. The teams travel hours by bus to play in tiny stadiums in front of a few hundred fans.

Still, Wright knew his assignment to the Appalachian League's Kingsport Mets was a necessary first step toward the majors. He knew thousands of young hopefuls had landed there before him. And he knew a lot of baseball dreams ended there.

Wright chose to focus his thoughts on a trio of Kingsport rookies who had gone before him: Darryl Strawberry, who played on four World Series Championship teams; Dwight Gooden, one of the most dominant National League pitchers of the mid- to late-1980s; and Kevin Mitchell, a two-time All-Star who played both infield and outfield. Wright wanted to add his name to that list. And he knew wishing alone wouldn't make it happen.

Wright stuck to the strategies that had gotten him this far: hard work, dedication, patience, and persistence. He proceeded to hit .300 with four home runs, 17 RBIs, and nine stolen bases in just 36 Appalachian League games. He quickly proved his value and was promoted to the Class A Capital City Bombers to start the 2002 season.

Wright's power appealed to Bombers fans in Columbia, South Carolina. As a 19-year-old, he batted .266 with 11 homers, 94 RBIs, and 21 stolen bases in 135 games. The statistics were impressive enough to earn him a spot in the South Atlantic League All-Star Game and, in 2003, an assignment with the Mets Class A Advanced squad in St. Lucie, Florida.

"I thought he was going to be real good," St. Lucie Mets manager Ken Oberkfell told MLB.com at the time. "He just stood out, he was a very good player. . . . I remember we had to shut him down from working out, he was working so much. He was always wanting to work and learn. . . . He had problems on and off defensively, but he worked on it. He worked to get better and he still works to stay that way."

While Wright was with St. Lucie, he met hitting instructor Howard Johnson, a former All-Star third baseman for the Mets who became the franchise's big-league hitting coach in 2007.

"He's taught me a lot," Wright told *MLB.com*. "We talk a lot about the mental side of hitting. I love just sitting down and talking to [Johnson] about hitting, defense, game situations."

The talks seem to have paid off. In 2003, Wright led the Florida State League with 72 walks, 56 extra-base hits, and 39 doubles. He also earned All-Star honors for the second consecutive year. He went on to finish ninth in the elite Arizona Fall League with a .341 batting average.

Wright kicked his career into high gear in 2004, rocketing through the upper levels of the minor leagues. He started the season in Binghamton, New York, with the Double-A

David Wright calls Howard Johnson (right), "the best hitting coach in the game." He told the New York Post: "I owe a lot to that man."

Binghamton Mets and, in mid-June, was promoted to the Triple-A Tides in Norfolk.

"David never looks for credit and he never, ever seeks attention," Joe Hietpas told *Sports Illustrated*. Catcher Hietpas and Wright were roommates when they played together on three different minor league teams. "Wherever he's played, he's been the most dedicated, the most motivated, the most enthusiastic."

That enthusiasm really shined through when Wright got the chance to play for his hometown Tides. He signed autographs and posed for photos, remembering the days — not so long ago — when he had been in the stands, longing for a chance to meet his sports heroes.

Fans love David Wright and he loves them back. He's become known for putting his glove on his head so that he can sign autographs.

"I remember as a kid going to see the Norfolk Tides and just screaming for autographs, screaming for anyone to acknowledge [me]," he told *Sports Illustrated*. "A majority of the players just walked by. I told myself if I was ever in that position, anytime I had the available time, I'd stop and sign."

Kindness counts, but Wright knew what really mattered was his athletic performance—and he delivered. In just 31 games, he hit .298 with eight homers and 17 RBIs. It was a feat that captured the attention of fans and Mets management alike.

On July 21, 2004, after only five weeks with the Tides, Wright was called up to the big leagues. He was finally a New York Met.

"I Want to Be a Met My Whole Career"

Wright may have been born in Virginia, but he quickly made New York his second home. In late 2007, he gave up a rented Upper East Side apartment and bought a $6 million Manhattan loft that's been decorated to his exact specifications.

"Just living here, I feel like I've become more cultured," he told *New York* magazine. "The museums, the people. In Virginia, where I grew up, it was a very conservative town. Just take the food in New York. I don't know if I'd ever had sushi before I came here, but in New York, every other place is a sushi restaurant."

He brags about the city's parks, architecture, arts scene, and, of course, its sports teams. "To me, New York is the greatest baseball stage in the world," he told *Sports Illustrated.* "The fans have a certain energy, a passion, a fire that I haven't seen anywhere else."

Wright is finally at home—both on and off the field.

"I want to be a Met my whole career," he told *Jets Insider.*

Joining the Mets in the middle of the season, he played just 69 games in 2004. It was a good introduction; he racked

David Wright's batting average took a nosedive in 2009. While critics tried to blame the slump on a variety of factors, Wright didn't want to talk about excuses. He simply wanted to start hitting the ball again.

up 77 hits, 14 home runs, and 40 RBIs. Over the next four seasons, the statistics continued to wow fans. He had 116 RBIs in 2006, a 2007 batting average of .325, and 33 homers in 2008. The numbers were impressive enough to win him both the National League Gold Glove Award and Silver Slugger Award for 2007 and 2008. He was also selected to the National League All-Star Team in 2006, 2007, and 2008.

Then, in 2009 — the Mets' first year in their new ballpark, Citi Field — Wright hit a slump. He went from knocking in 124 RBIs in 2008 to a disappointing 72 in 2009. He recorded a career-low 10 home runs, and was put on the disabled list (DL) for 15 days after being hit in the head with a pitch.

It was a setback, but one that Wright met straight on. He spent the 2009–2010 off-season shuttling between his homes in New York and Virginia, but he also spent considerable time in Florida, working with batting coach Johnson. He watched videos, took extra batting practices, and actually studied the physics of his swing. He even got to a point where he could see the positive side of being on the DL.

"Just watching the game has allowed me to learn a lot about what goes on . . . what we need to do more as a team successfully."

"Just watching the game has allowed me to learn a lot about what goes on, seeing things from a different perspective, what we can improve on, what we need to do more as a team successfully," he told MLB.com.

Wright headed into the 2010 spring training armed with both self-assurance and optimism.

"I'm ready to go," he told the *New York Post*. "I'm excited. We have a lot to prove. I have some things to prove."

Fans and sports analysts alike are drawn to that confident, can-do attitude. Teammates, too, respect the player who, despite his young age, is comfortable assuming a leadership role on the team. For example, when Brian Schneider was traded to the Mets in 2008, he got the expected phone call from Mets General Manager Omar Minaya.

David Wright is a player's player. When the Mets signed Johan Santana in 2008, Wright was the only player on stage with him for the official announcement.

Almost as soon as he and Minaya hung up, he received a text message from one of his new teammates: David Wright.

"It was like right away," Schneider told *The New York Times*. "I'm barely on the team and he's already reaching out. Shows what kind of guy he is."

Wright says he only wants to do what he can to make new team members feel comfortable.

"No matter how many years of experience you have in baseball, it's a different experience in New York," Wright told *The New York Times*. "Am I a salty veteran? Absolutely not. But I do have a little bit of knowledge of what to expect."

He hopes to become the kind of mentor his more experienced teammates — veterans like infielder Todd Zeile and pitchers Al Leiter, John Franco, and Tom Glavine — were to him when he first joined the team.

> "People say there's a lot of pressure here, but thats what I live for. No one puts more pressure on me than I do."

"People say there's a lot of pressure here, but that's what I live for," Wright told *New York* magazine. "No one puts more pressure on me than I do. It's important to be a leader, especially to the younger guys. . . . It feels weird to say that. I mean, just a couple years ago, I was one of them. I guess, in a way, I still am."

David Wright (right) has often been compared to New York Yankees shortstop Derek Jeter (left). They were both chosen for the 2009 World Baseball Classic. Team USA lost to Japan in the tournament semifinal.

Character Counts

"**I**f you were going to start from scratch and design the perfect New York ballplayer, David Wright is the kid you'd come up with," former Mets third baseman Howard Johnson told *Sports Illustrated*. "New Yorkers feel cheated if you don't play hard, get dirty and spill some blood. That's what the shortstop on the Yankees does, and that's what David Wright does."

The Yankees shortstop to whom Johnson refers is Derek Jeter. He's not the first to compare the two ballplayers. Sportswriters love to point out the pair's similar skill, good looks, and charisma.

When he was growing up, Wright says he admired Cal Ripken Jr., but since moving to New York, Jeter has become his role model. "[Jeter has] offered me some great advice," he told *New York* magazine. "He just says to remember who you were when you started and don't change. It sounds simple, but it's not. You wear the uniform, you're under a microscope."

While the romances, partying, and public tantrums of many sports stars make headlines, Wright maintains a relatively low-key, clean image. He goes to clubs and has fun, but he balances that by striving to be the kind of person kids can look up to.

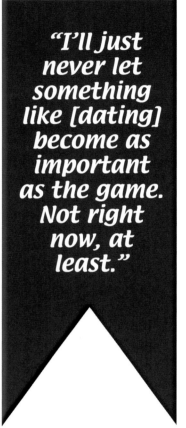

"I'll just never let something like [dating] become as important as the game. Not right now, at least."

"I have to remember, baseball is the reason I have my apartment, baseball is the reason I'm on the cover of video games—baseball is what I do," he told *New York* magazine. "I'm not saying I don't ever . . . I mean, I go on dates, but I'll just never let something like that become as important as the game. Not right now, at least."

He channels his off-the-field energies into competitions of all sorts: paintball battles, video game showdowns, bowling matchups, pickup basketball games, and more. Wright cherishes the opportunity to compete with teammates, friends, and—perhaps most of all—his three younger brothers, Stephen, Daniel, and Matt. The siblings are always trying to beat each other at wrestling, basketball, video games, darts, football—you name it, they've probably challenged each other at it.

"They even compete when they eat," their father, Rhon, told *Jets Insider*. Whether it's a contest to see who can eat the most rolls in a minute or who can burp the loudest, these guys love to challenge one another.

That fire-in-the-belly spark is part of Wright's allure. He smiles at fans. He runs onto the field. He doesn't even mind the jokes about how he sticks his tongue out when he's really concentrating on something.

Referred to as the "face" of the New York Mets, David Wright's fame reaches beyond sports fans. He's a popular guest on talk shows and is often featured in magazines.

"There have been other kids in our organization who you latch on to and like, but then, for whatever reason, they didn't make it," Mets Chief Operating Officer Jeff Wilpon told *New York* magazine. "David is the exception. I've been lucky enough to meet guys like Michael Jordan and Wayne Gretzky, and I believe David has that thing, you know, that same approach to the game that made them so addicting to watch."

Wright's celebrity status is rising at a rate not often seen in baseball. Before he reached 30, he had already appeared on the covers of *ESPN Magazine*, *Men's Health*, *Play*, and *The Sporting News*. He's had inside features and photo spreads in

Cosmopolitan, GQ, Sports Illustrated, and *People.* In 2007, he became the first Mets player to be immortalized in wax at Madame Tussauds in New York. He's traded baseball stories with President George W. Bush at the White House, laughed it up with David Letterman on late-night TV, and offered personal batting lessons to comedian Jerry Seinfeld and actor Matthew Broderick.

> **"I've never put anything illegal into my body. I take a lot of pride in that."**

Likable as he is, Wright is willing to take on the media—and the fans—if his reputation is at stake. When his stats took a downward turn in 2009, there were those who suggested his earlier performance may have been boosted by steroids. Outraged, he addressed the allegations head on: "Since I came into the league, we've had drug tests," he told the *New York Post.* "Major League Baseball, the Players Association, we've got great drug testing going on. And I think that speaks for itself. I've never put anything illegal into my body. I take a lot of pride in that."

Twins first baseman and fellow Virginian Mike Cuddyer was Wright's minor league teammate and roommate. He says Wright's greatest strengths are his character and his ability to know right from wrong.

"I don't care what anybody says, we are role models and David knows it's important to be a good role model," Cuddyer told *Jets Insider.* In an interview with the *New York Times,* Mets veteran Billy Wagner summed up Wright this way: "He's well mannered, he's well liked, he's well disciplined and he's well rounded."

Giving Back

Wright believes strongly in giving back to the people and the communities that have supported him along the way. After just a year in the majors, he started his own charity: The David Wright Foundation. The organization's initial purpose was to improve the lives of children suffering from multiple sclerosis. Its first event was a gala dinner at the New York Stock Exchange Member's Club that raised more than $100,000 for several New York–area multiple sclerosis centers.

Since then, the foundation has expanded its scope. It provides aid and assistance to children in need, working with a variety of charitable organizations including the Make-a-Wish Foundation, United States Marine Corps' Toys for Tots, Boys and Girls Club, Kids in Crisis, Fresh Air Fund, Tuesday's Children, The New York University Hospital Neonatal Intensive Care Unit, Harlem Children's Zone, Boys Hope Girls Hope, and Children's Village. As a tribute to his police officer father, the David Wright Foundation also partners with the Police Athletic League and the Patrolman's Benevolent Association.

American Idol winner David Cook teaches Wright to drum at the 2008 "Do the Wright Thing" gala. David Wright's galas attract big stars from sports, music, television, and movies. The events raise money for children in need.

Baseball gloves, bats, books, computers, dance classes, homework clubs, medical care, and day camps are just a sampling of the goods and services that Wright's foundation has been able to provide to children—primarily in New York and Virginia.

He's also been a proud participant in Major League Baseball's Welcome Back Veterans program, a series of events and initiatives that addresses the mental health and job needs of U.S. veterans returning from overseas.

Wright's many philanthropic works have been recognized. He's won the Thurman Munson humanitarian award and the Sports Humanitarian Award from the New Jersey Sports Writers Association.

David Wright, left, took on Yankee Derek Jeter in Delta Airlines' 2009 Batting Challenge. The two are friends, but were happy to slug it out in an effort to raise money for their charities.

"I have been blessed with the ability to play this game I love so much," Wright said in his MLB.com biography. "But I was taught that with great power comes great responsibility. I feel it is my duty to give 100 percent on the field and to give back to the people of this city who have given me so much."

In 2009, Wright and Jeter partnered up for Delta Airlines' Batting Challenge. The season-long event promised $100,000 to the charity of the player with the highest batting average. Jeter edged out Wright with a .334 batting average over Wright's .307. Of course, Wright wanted to win, but he was

Former Mets general manager Willie Randolph, rear right, and mascot Mr. Met accompany David Wright as he portrays Santa during a visit to deliver gifts to schoolchildren in New York City.

still very happy to be able to add the $50,000 runner's-up prize to his foundation's account.

For Wright, the foundation is about much more than just hanging out with celebrities and raising money at fancy parties. He likes to walk the walk, showing up at community centers to play video games with kids after school, or signing autographs for children in the hospital.

Just before Thanksgiving in 2008, the third baseman visited patients at Children's Hospital of The King's Daughters (CHKD) in Hampton Roads, Virginia. He stopped by to drop off a check for $25,000, which would go toward creating a video game and movie library that would help keep hospital-bound kids entertained. He's also visited the hospital at Christmastime to personally deliver toys to children.

CHKD Executive Medical Director Dr. Albert Finch said Wright's visits to children suffering from cancer, sickle cell disease, and a host of other illnesses go a long way toward lifting spirits. "He brought four carloads of toys with him," Finch said in a news release posted on the hospital's web site. "He was incredibly generous, bringing gifts for children of all ages and making sure to select the perfect gift for each child. And he was just as generous with his time as he made his way from room to room. Not only that, but he brought close friends and family with him to share the experience of making a truly special day for hospitalized children on Christmas Eve. It was quite touching for everyone associated with CHKD."

> "[David] brought four carloads of toys with him. . . . He was just as generous with his time as he made his way from room to room."

Wright insists that the time he spends visiting hospitals is just as inspiring for him. Of a visit to the Gimbel Multiple Sclerosis Comprehensive Care Center at Holy Name Hospital in Teaneck, New Jersey, he told MLB.com: "I think I ended up getting more out of it than the patients did. It was an amazing experience and it made me want to do more."

Whether he's swinging a baseball bat, lifting weights in the off-season, or visiting children, the idea of "doing more" drives Wright. He is, after all, a talented, respectful, hardworking player who clearly is the "Wright" fit for Mets fans.

1982	David Allen Wright is born December 20 to Rhon and Elisa Wright in Norfolk, Virginia.
1999	He earns Virginia High School Baseball Coaches Association All-State honors.
2000	He earns All-State honors again.
2001	Wright is named Gatorade Virginia Baseball Player of the Year and Virginia High School Coaches Association Player of the Year, and he earns All-State honors again. He is chosen in the first round of the Major League Baseball draft.
2002	He is promoted to the Class A Capital City Bombers.
2003	He is promoted to the Mets Class A Advanced team.
2004	Wright makes his major league debut on July 21. Online voters award him MLB.com's Rookie of the Year Award.
2005	He establishes the David Wright Foundation to provide financial support for those in need. Online voters select his barehanded catch in an August 9 game against the San Diego Padres as MLB.com's Play of the Year.
2006	Delta Airlines names one of its planes The Wright Flight in his honor. Wright is selected to MLB's National League All-Star Team.
2007	He meets President George W. Bush at a White House dinner on February 5. He is selected for the All-Star Team again. He wins the National League Gold Glove Award for superior fielding and the National League Silver Slugger Award for outstanding offensive play.
2008	For the third year in a row, he is selected for the All-Star Team. He again wins the National League Gold Glove Award and the National League Silver Slugger Award. He joins Johnny Damon of the Yankees, Brandon Webb of the Diamondbacks, and Albert Pujols of the Cardinals as nominees for the Roberto Clemente Award for humanitarian service. He wins the New Jersey Sports Writers Association Sports Humanitarian Award. He wins the Thurman Munson Award for excellence in both athletic competition and philanthropic work.

2009   Wright makes his 836th career start at third base, the most starts at the position in Mets franchise history. He hits the first Mets home run in Citi Field history on April 13. He is selected for the All-Star Team, and as a representative of the USA Team in the World Baseball Classic. He suffers a concussion when Matt Cain of the San Francisco Giants hits him in the head with a 94-mile-per-hour fastball on August 15.

2010   At 27 years and 127 days old, Wright becomes the youngest ever Mets player to reach 1,000 hits on April 27. He reached the feat in his 868th career game, quicker than any other Met in history.

Major League Statistics

SEASON	TEAM	G	AB	R	H	2B	3B	HR	RBI	SB	AVG
2004	NY Mets	69	263	41	77	17	1	14	40	6	.293
2005	NY Mets	160	575	99	176	42	1	27	102	17	.306
2006	NY Mets	154	582	96	181	40	5	26	116	20	.311
2007	NY Mets	160	604	113	196	42	1	30	107	34	.325
2008	NY Mets	160	626	115	189	42	2	33	124	15	.302
2009	NY Mets	144	535	88	164	39	3	10	72	27	.307
Career Totals		847	3,185	552	983	222	13	140	561	119	.309

G—Games; AB—At-Bats; R—Runs; H—Hits; 2B—Doubles; 3B—Triples; HR—Home Runs; RBI—Runs Batted In; SB—Stolen Bases; AVG—Batting Average

FURTHER READING

Books

Gitlin, Marty. *David Wright: Gifted and Giving Baseball Star.* Berkeley Heights, N.J.: Enslow Publishers, 2010.

Stewart, Mark. *The New York Mets.* Chicago: Norwood House Press, 2008.

Works Consulted

Amsden, David. "Mr. Clean." *New York*, April 1, 2007, http://nymag.com/news/features/30019/

Botte, Peter. "New York Mets Third Baseman David Wright Calls for HGH Blood Testing in Major League Baseball." *New York Daily News*, January 14, 2010, http://www.nydailynews.com/sports/baseball/mets/2010/01/14/2010-01-14_calls_for_game_to_get_tough.html

Children's Hospital of the King's Daughters http://www.chkd.org/

Costa, Brian. "Q&A: New York Mets' David Wright, New York Yankees' Derek Jeter Talk about Each Other." *NJ.com*, posted on June 12, 2009, http://www.nj.com/mets/index.ssf/2009/06/qa_new_york_mets_david_wright.html

"Doin' the Wright Thing: Mayor Pavia Announces Two Grants From New York Mets Superstar David Wright," news release issued by City of Stamford, Connecticut, on January 7, 2010.

Emrich, Robert. "Path of the Pros: David Wright." *MLB.com*, posted on December 17, 2009, http://web.minorleaguebaseball.com/news/article.jsp?ymd=20091101&content_id=7595840&vkey=news_milb&fext=.jsp

"Great David Wright," *Jets Insider*, posted on January 8, 2006, http://www.jetsinsider.com/forums/showthread.php?t=118513

Hale, Mark. "Mets' Wright Expects to Bounce Back in 2010." *New York Post*, January 8, 2010, http://www.nypost.com/p/sports/mets/wright_man_for_the_job_kXTWo2CLhlCo4zSu97YX4K

Jenkins, Lee. "Virginia's Boy Wonders." *Sports Illustrated* (SI Vault), September 29, 2008, http://sportsillustrated.cnn.com/vault/article/magazine/MAG1145707/index.htm

Lidz, Frank. "Prince of the City." *Sports Illustrated* (SI Vault), May 29, 2006,
http://sportsillustrated.cnn.com/vault/article/magazine/MAG1111424/index.htm

Noble, Marty, and Jesse Sanchez. "Wright's 836th Start at Third a Mets Record." MLB.com, posted on September 26, 2009,
http://www.mlb.com/news/article.jsp?ymd=20090925&content_id=7159996&vkey=news_nym&c_id=nym

Perkins, Owen. "Wright Sports New Helmet in Return." MLB.com, posted on September 2, 2009,
http://www.mlb.com/news/article.jsp?ymd=20090901&content_id=6737876&vkey=news_nym&c_id=nym

Shpigel, Ben. "Baseball Actively Promotes Him, Advertisers Eagerly Chase After Him." *The New York Times*, April 1, 2007,
http://www.nytimes.com/2007/04/01/sports/baseball/01mets.html
———. "Meet David Wright, the Real Mr. Met." *The New York Times*, February 10, 2008,
http://www.nytimes.com/2008/02/10/sports/baseball/10mets.html

Syken, Bill. "2 New York Mets: Rising Star David Wright Spearheads a Shea Resurgence." *Sports Illustrated* (SI Vault), April 3, 2006,
http://sportsillustrated.cnn.com/vault/article/magazine/MAG1110398/index.htm

"Wright Now: The Official MLB Blog of David Wright," posted on May 24, 2006,
http://tinyurl.com/yjmfzdy

On the Internet

Baseball-Reference.com — Baseball Statistics and History
http://www.baseball-reference.com

David Wright Foundation
http://mlb.mlb.com/players/david_wright/foundation

David Wright — Official Site
http://www.mlb.com/players/david_wright/

INDEX